STEWART FERRIS

summersdale

CELEBRITY CHAT-UP LINES
Copyright © Stewart Ferris 2006

The right of Stewart Ferris to be identified as the author of
this work has been asserted in accordance with sections 77
and 78 of the Copyright, Designs and Patents Act 1988.

Summersdale Publishers Ltd
46 West Street
Chichester
West Sussex
PO19 1RP
UK

www.summersdale.com

ISBN: 1-84024-540-9
ISBN: 978-1-84024-540-0

Printed and bound in Great Britain.

Important note:

This is *not* a book of quotations from celebrities. None of the celebrities listed in this book have endorsed or approved this book, nor have they ever said or written the chat-up lines that are beneath their names. These chat-up lines are written by the author, Stewart Ferris, in a style parodying the celebrities as portrayed in their works or in the media. In other words, it's just a bit of fun...

A suggested chat-up line for:

Peter Andre

Hey baby, let me show you my six-pack. It's in the shopping bag, under all the pies.

A suggested chat-up line for:

David Beckham

If you come closer I'll
show you how much I
can bend it.

A suggested chat-up line for:

Kate Beckinsale

Never mind Pearl
Harbor, how about you
give me a pearl
necklace?

A suggested chat-up line for:

Sarah Beeny

You look pretty nicely refurbished. Can I check out your pipework?

A suggested chat-up line for:

Halle Berry

If I said I had a beautiful body would you hold it against you?

A suggested chat-up line for:

Cilla Black

You chose number two, our lovely Cilla from Liverpool.

A suggested chat-up line for:

Tony Blair

I used to be head of a country of sixty million people. Could you give head as big as that?

A suggested chat-up line for:

Brian Blessed

I'm an experienced actor, my dear, so I can assure you I know how to play the role of a great lover.

A suggested chat-up line for:

Bono

With you I think I've finally found what I'm looking for. Mind you, I probably would have found it a few years sooner if I'd taken off my sunglasses so I could see what I was doing.

A suggested chat-up line for:

Richard Branson

What sort of thing do you look for in a millionaire… ahem, I mean, in a man?

A suggested chat-up line for:

Dan Brown

Solve the anagram codes in this sentence: 'You have nice *sitt*; I want to *hags* you.'

A suggested chat-up line for:

Pete Burns

Why don't we snuggle beneath this entirely legal fur coat which is definitely not made from any endangered species, and in particular is not made of gorilla fur?

A suggested chat-up line for:

Paul Burrell

Let me show you why
Diana thought of me as
her 'rock'.

A suggested chat-up line for:

George W. Bush

Any of you folks
wanna see my
nucular warhead?

A suggested chat-up line for:

Vicki Butler-Henderson

I'd like to look under your bonnet, wipe your dipstick, take you for a test drive and see if I can park you in my garage.

A suggested chat-up line for:

Michael Caine

Is that an Oscar in my pocket or am I just pleased to see you?

A suggested chat-up line for:

David Cameron

I've got a photo of
Tony Blair in my pants:
have a look and tell me
which is the biggest
prick you see.

A suggested chat-up line for:

Naomi Campbell

I'm a model. A top of the range model, in fact, but I still need a good servicing.

A suggested chat-up line for:

Kerry Catona

Big, aren't they?
Touch them,
they're real.
I got them at Iceland.

A suggested chat-up line for:

Jackie Chan

When I first went to
Hollywood my English wasn't
so good so instead of studying
martial arts I accidentally
enrolled in a course
for *marital* arts. Lucky you.

A suggested chat-up line for:

Chantelle

Hey, I'm in a book of celebrity chat-up lines. That's my claim to fame. If that doesn't make you fancy me I don't know what will.

A suggested chat-up line for:

Prince Charles

One may look like a
dinosaur and think like
a dinosaur, but one is
hung like one too.

A suggested chat-up line for:

Cher

Make me hot, baby.
But not too hot –
I'm highly flammable.

A suggested chat-up line for:

Charlotte Church

Why don't you slip into my confessional and tell me what a bad boy you've been?

A suggested chat-up line for:

Jeremy Clarkson

You're not American, are you? You don't drive an American car or watch *Friends*? Thank goodness for that. Let me buy you a British drink.

A suggested chat-up line for:

Julian Clary

Would you like to come caving with me? I'm sure we could have fun squeezing into tight crevices.

A suggested chat-up line for:

John Cleese

You want to see me do a silly walk? Give me one night with you and we'll both have trouble walking straight.

A suggested chat-up line for:

Martin Clunes

You'd make a great booby prize. Mind if I have a lucky dip?

A suggested chat-up line for:

Sean Connery

You won't be able to reshisht my shecret weapon: women adore my shpeech impediment.

A suggested chat-up line for:

Steve Coogan

Knowing me, Steve Coogan, knowing you, whatever your name is. Aha.

A suggested chat-up line for:

Simon Cowell

I think you've presented yourself badly. Frankly, you look awful. Your hair's a mess, your voice sounds like a cat being strangled and you smell like you've been muckspreading on a farm. But I've had worse, so you're through to my dating shortlist.

A suggested chat-up line for:

Sara Cox

You'll be pleased to know that my name reflects my main interest in life, actually, and it's a mis-spelling, of course. It should really be spelt 'Sarah'.

A suggested chat-up line for:

Daniel Craig

Stand back and
watch my gadget
pop out, baby.

A suggested chat-up line for:

Paul Daniels

I can bring pleasure
to any woman,
simply by making
myself disappear.

A suggested chat-up line for:

Julia Davis

You make me feel all maternal. I think I'd like to have your baby. How much do you want for him?

A suggested chat-up line for:

Angus Deayton

Have I got news for you, sweetheart – it's your lucky day. Before we go any further, do you take Visa?

A suggested chat-up line for:

Judi Dench

When I pick a man for an important mission he has to understand the risks. I expect him to go down for me if necessary.

A suggested chat-up line for:

Charlie Dimmock

I've trimmed my herbaceous border, plucked out the weeds and mowed the lawn. I look great in a bikini now. Get undressed too so you can sow some seeds with me.

A suggested chat-up line for:

James Dyson

If you're wondering where I got the idea for the extendable hose on my vacuum cleaners, let me show you.

A suggested chat-up line for:

Noel Edmonds

It's easy to confuse me with a banker, but that's not me. I'm the one who wants you to open your box for me.

A suggested chat-up line for:

Chris Eubank

It ith with the utmotht rethpect that I pwethent to you my perthonage for the purpothe of wooing you.

A suggested chat-up line for:

Chris Evans

I never thought I'd say
this, but I'm saying it now:
I wish I'd kept my clothes
on when I presented *TFI
Friday*, 'cos now there'll be
no nice surprises when I
take you home.

A suggested chat-up line for:

Mohamed Al-Fayed

I run a corner shop so you can rely on me to fulfil your every desire.

A suggested chat-up line for:

Vanessa Feltz

Love me for who I am
inside, for beneath my
spacious exterior lies
a very thin lady who
likes eating pies.

A suggested chat-up line for:

Bruce Forsyth

I know what you're thinking, and the answer's yes: chin length is a good indication.

A suggested chat-up line for:

Calista
Flockhart

I'm cooking a lettuce leaf tonight. Wanna share it with me?

A suggested chat-up line for:

Martin Freeman

I had a big part in *The Office*, but I'd like to have an even bigger part in you.

A suggested chat-up line for:

Dawn French

How would I
describe myself?
Well-upholstered,
a kind of Dawn French
lookalike.

A suggested chat-up line for:

Bill Gates

I think you'll be pretty impressed with what I can do with my hard drive. Until it crashes, of course.

A suggested chat-up line for:

Uri Geller

I'm famous for making
things go limp
when I rub them.
Hopefully you'll have
the opposite effect.

A suggested chat-up line for:

Ricky Gervais

You're probably thinking,
'What's a good-looking
guy like me doing in a
place like this?' yeah? Fact.
I'm here for the local
beauties. Women. Not in a
sexist way. And not that

men aren't beautiful.
Some men are gorgeous.
Big muscles. Not for me,
I'm straight. Designer
stubble can look good.
I could shag every woman
here. Shaved chest.
If they'd let me, yeah.
Six-pack stomachs.

A suggested chat-up line for:

Gary Glitter

Can I help you with
your homework?

A suggested chat-up line for:

Jade Goody

Are you Bri'ish or are you from East Angular? Eh? I like a quiet man who lets me do the gabbin'. Yeah. 'Ello? Oi, say summink. Oh, you're a shop dummy.

A suggested chat-up line for:

Hugh Grant

I, I, I wonder if you would do me the honour of, of, of giving me something in, in, in return for money… like, like, like stutter therapy.

A suggested chat-up line for:

Geri Halliwell

If you can eat a vindaloo
without sweating then
you're my man –
I'm the hottest spice
on the planet.

A suggested chat-up line for:

Tom Hanks

Have you ever
done it with the world's
biggest movie star?
Wanna do it with
me too?

A suggested chat-up line for:

Rolf Harris

I know what you're thinking, but that's not my extra leg.

A suggested chat-up line for:

Prince Harry

Hi, I'm a prince. Let me take you back to my castle and show you the size of my turret.

A suggested chat-up line for:

Stephen Hawking

My voice is mechanically
enhanced. My legs are
mechanically enhanced. I
don't think you need a brain
as big as mine to see where
this is going…

A suggested chat-up line for:

Tim Henman

The score between us is love all. How about we take it all the way to your advantage?

A suggested chat-up line for:

Lenny Henry

Have you ever done it with a love machine, baby? I have, and it's kick-ass: I'll lend it to you when I'm done with it.

A suggested chat-up line for:

Paris Hilton

I used to be called Bognor Bed and Breakfast, but I wanted to sound more luxurious. Would you like to see my facilities? Oh, I forgot, the whole world's already seen them.

A suggested chat-up line for:

Ian Hislop

Women love it when I
try to chat them up.
They enjoy the breeze
on their ankles.

A suggested chat-up line for:

Ron Howard

Hi, I'm a big shot movie director but you probably remember me from that seventies sitcom back when I had hair. I can certainly offer you some *Happy Days*, baby.

A suggested chat-up line for:

Michael Jackson

I was found completely innocent of all charges of being a freak, so why not come and take a bath with me? It's full of Bubbles, but he won't mind sharing.

A suggested chat-up line for:

Mick Jagger

I used to take brown sugar, then white sugar, but at my age I'm quite satisfied without any sugar at all. I still love shagging, though.

A suggested chat-up line for:

David Jason

Would you like to see
my plonker? He's over
there.

A suggested chat-up line for:

Elton John

Come upstairs with me and I'll sing you *Rocket Man*. Don't make me burn my fuse up there alone.

A suggested chat-up line for:

Ulrika Jonsson

I'm not afraid of commitment: I love being married. That's why I do it so often.

A suggested chat-up line for:

Tom Jones

Do you have any Welsh in you? Would you like some?

A suggested chat-up line for:

Jordan

'Yes' is the favourite word I know. It's also one of the longest.

A suggested chat-up line for:

Jude Law

If you're a <u>Law</u>-abiding citizen, then do as I say and kiss me.

A suggested chat-up line for:

Laurence Llewelyn-Bowen

I'm rather fussy about style when it comes to lovers. My ideal match would have to have long dark hair, frilly cuffs and a smart purple velvet outfit. Oh, that's me, isn't it?

A suggested chat-up line for:

Andrew Lloyd Webber

I'm rather fond of a pussy or two. That's why I wrote *Cats*.

A suggested chat-up line for:

Matt Lucas

I'm not related to George, but I do have a pretty impressive light sabre.

A suggested chat-up line for:

Joanna Lumley

Darling, as Patsy might say, after you've had Keith Moon, everyone's an improvement.

A suggested chat-up line for:

Ellen MacArthur

I got a big thrill from sailing round the world single-handed. Can you do anything with one hand that would thrill me more?

A suggested chat-up line for:

Madonna

I love Englishmen
with their locks, their
stocks and their
smoking barrels.

A suggested chat-up line for:

Barry Manilow

You should put up your umbrella now, sweetheart. I think I'm gonna sneeze.

A suggested chat-up line for:

Rik Mayall

Well, baby, are you pleased to see me or have I got a giant ego in my pocket?

A suggested chat-up line for:

Davina McCall

I like all men to be as big as my brother.

A suggested chat-up line for:

Paul McCartney

How about I drive
my yellow submarine
up your long and
winding road?

A suggested chat-up line for:

Paul McKenna

Relax, follow my hand... you are very sleepy... you are under my control... forget everything you used to think about men... now you think men without hair are the sexiest thing on the planet. And open your eyes!

A suggested chat-up line for:

George Michael

Hi! Mind if I join you in there? Just slide the lock to 'vacant'.

A suggested chat-up line for:

Kate Moss

I need someone who
can handle my
peculiarities.
Here, have a try...

A suggested chat-up line for:

Andy Murray

You've heard of Henman Hill: now it's called Murray Mount. Let me show you how it works...

A suggested chat-up line for:

Graham Norton

I'm a regular on Radio 4's *Just A Minute*, so you probably know that I can't keep it up for as long as sixty seconds.

A suggested chat-up line for:

Jamie Oliver

Open your mouth and
prepare for a treat:
I can whip up
something tasty for you.

A suggested chat-up line for:

Kelly Osbourne

Shut up and get in my f★!#ing bed now, you #★!^%$ @{}★<>&$★!

A suggested chat-up line for:

Kelly Osbourne

Shut up and get in my f*!#ing bed now, you #*!^%$ @{}*<>&$*!

A suggested chat-up line for:

Tara Palmer-Tomkinson

I'm prepared to work hard at our relationship. Provided 'hard work' means never having to do anything ever, not having to have heard of *Steptoe and Son*, and being invited to posh parties.

A suggested chat-up line for:

Nicholas Parsons

I'm going to talk to you for one minute about why I'm the sale of the century.

A suggested chat-up line for:

Billie Piper

My box might look small on the outside, but you can fit a whole ward full of doctors on the inside.

A suggested chat-up line for:

The Queen

One takes it up the
annus horribilis,
you know.

A suggested chat-up line for:

Cliff Richard

People wouldn't call me the Peter Pan of pop if they saw the size of my hook...

A suggested chat-up line for:

Anne Robinson

I suppose you're expecting me to make some lame quip about looking for the weakest link in my bra strap or something. Pathetic.

A suggested chat-up line for:

Tony Robinson

I present *Time Team* so
I'm very good at
squeezing myself into
damp holes.

A suggested chat-up line for:

Jonathan Ross

I've weached a senior
wank at the BBC, so I
weally fink that we should
stwip naked and wun
awound the woom weally
wapidly to celebwate.

A suggested chat-up line for:

Jennifer Saunders

If I give you my mobile number will you promise to call me? Just give me long enough to set it to vibrate and stick it in my Lacroix panties.

A suggested chat-up line for:

Jimmy Saville

I could fix it for you to get an hour of pure ecstasy in bed. Then, when you're done, perhaps I could join you?

A suggested chat-up line for:

Michael Schumacher

If it's Teutonic sausage you're after, you'd better let me into your cockpit. I can be in and out of your pitstop in less than ten seconds.

A suggested chat-up line for:

William Shatner

Brace yourself, baby:
my phaser's set to stun.

A suggested chat-up line for:

Ned Sherrin

I'm fed up with being at a loose end. Can I try your other end?

A suggested chat-up line for:

Ringo Starr

Ignore Brucie: it's nose size that counts. But don't be nervous – I'm sure my tank engine will fit nicely in your sidings.

A suggested chat-up line for:

Sting

Let me teach you all I know about tantric lovemaking. Assuming you have five minutes to spare, of course.

A suggested chat-up line for:

Janet
Street-Porter

I happen to be quite a
media mogul, even
though I may look
like a media mongrel.

A suggested chat-up line for:

Alan Sugar

You've been coming on to me all evening, but I'm not impressed with your small talk, your charisma or your body. I've a good mind to dump you. Give me three good reasons why I should sleep with you.

A suggested chat-up line for:

Chris Tarrant

You have the option to
phone a friend. I like a
threesome.

A suggested chat-up line for:

Catherine Tate

Would I like to go on
top? Am I bovvered?

A suggested chat-up line for:

Margaret Thatcher

I may be an iron lady but I'm not rusty where it counts. Best bring some 3-in-1 oil, though, just to be on the safe side.

A suggested chat-up line for:

Alan Titchmarsh

I have a favourite perennial that pops up when it gets warm and, although it can get pretty big, it's best not to prune it.

A suggested chat-up line for:

Abi Titmuss

My best features are reflected in my name because I have two admirable protrusions. Just like Westminster Abbey.

A suggested chat-up line for:

Carol Vorderman

I've calculated our symmetry and my findings reflect a high probability that you're coming home with me tonight.

A suggested chat-up line for:

Louis Walsh

I have to disagree with Simon. I think you're a great talent and I'd like to offer you a seedy deal. I mean a CD deal.

A suggested chat-up line for:

Robbie Williams

You know who I am.
I don't need a
chat-up line.

A suggested chat-up line for:

Venus Williams

Could I have new balls, please? I think I've worn out the old ones.

A suggested chat-up line for:

Barbara Windsor

Ooh, blimey, you make me
smash hits tingle, you make
me Berkshire Hunt flow like
the River Thames and you
make me evening tipples stand
to attention. Giggle, giggle.

A suggested chat-up line for:

Oprah Winfrey

Let me take you out to dinner. I know a great little place that's perfect for my diet. They serve yo-yos.

A suggested chat-up line for:

Michael Winner

I don't usually wear a dress.
Only if it's for a commercial.
OK, if you insist, I'll wear
one for you tonight. Hold my
zimmer frame while I
change...

A suggested chat-up line for:

Terry Wogan

I'll be thinking about you next time I have a blankety-blank.

A suggested chat-up line for:

Catherine Zeta-Jones

I'm the kind of girl who gets into a sticky situation whenever she handles a sword.

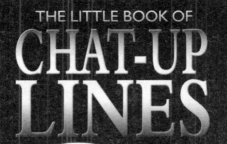

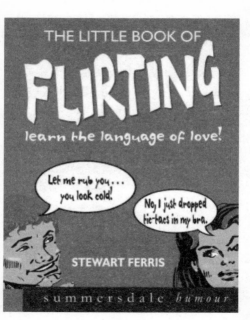

HOW TO CHAT-UP
BABES

Your place or mine?

You go to yours...
I'll go to mine.

STEWART FERRIS

summersdale *humour*

www.summersdale.com